Following God's Pattern
A Study of the Institutional Issues

by Roger Hillis

ONE STONE
BIBLICAL RESOURCES

Published by:
One Stone Press
979 Lovers Lane
Bowling Green, KY 42103

Printed in the United States of America

ISBN: 978-1-941422-41-0

ONE STONE
BIBLICAL RESOURCES

www.onestone.com

Table of Contents

Why Are We Divided?

In this first lesson, we need to study and discuss biblical teaching on the subject of division. It is certainly true that God hates division and those who cause division are condemned in the Bible (Proverbs 6:16-19). But is division always wrong? Will "the spirit of Christ" always prevent division, no matter what the issue? Or are there times when division is necessary? If so, how can that be determined and how can one know if he is the cause or the victim of division?

Is division necessarily bad?

The word "church" is from the Greek word *ekklesia* which means called out. We are called out of the world. "He has delivered us from the power of darkness and conveyed us into the kingdom of the Son of His love" (Colossians 1:13). James 4:4 teaches that those who are a friend of the world are the enemies of God. And Peter teaches that we are called out of darkness into light. "But you are a chosen generation, a royal priesthood, a holy nation, His own special people, that you may proclaim the praises of Him who called you out of darkness into His marvelous light" (1 Peter 2:9). Therefore, we are divided from the world and that is what God requires.

A stand for the truth may result in family division. "Do you suppose that I came to give peace on earth? I tell you, not at all, but rather division. For from now on five in one house will be divided: three against two, and two against three. Father will be divided against son and son against father, mother against daughter and daughter against mother, mother-in-law against her daughter-in-law and daughter-in-law against her mother-in-law" (Luke 12:51-53; see also Matthew 10:34-37).

> ...do you not know that **friendship** with the **world** is **hostility** toward **God**? Therefore whoever wishes to be a **friend** of the world makes himself an **enemy** of God.
>
> - James 4:4

> If anyone comes to you and **does not bring** this teaching, do not **receive** him into your **house**, and do not give him a **greeting**; for the one who gives him a greeting **participates** in his **evil deeds**.
>
> - 2 John 10-11

God authorizes separation of the pure and the impure within the church. "In the name of our Lord Jesus Christ, when you are gathered together, along with my spirit, with the power of our Lord Jesus Christ, deliver such a one to Satan for the destruction of the flesh, that his spirit may be saved in the day of the Lord Jesus...Therefore, put away from yourselves the evil person" (1 Corinthians 5:4-5, 13). "But we command you, brethren, in the name of our Lord Jesus Christ, that you withdraw from every brother who walks disorderly and not according to the tradition which he received from us" (2 Thessalonians 3:6).

Those who teach false doctrine must not be tolerated. "Now I urge you, brethren, note those who cause divisions and offenses, contrary to the doctrine which you learned, and avoid them" (Romans 16:17; see also 1 John 4:1 and 2 John 9-11.) It is just as wrong to encourage or support this person ("bid him God speed"—KJV) as it is to participate yourself in teaching false doctrine.

Division and separation are not always wrong. Division is sometimes commanded by God. Division is wrong if it is not over doctrinal matters. What God wants, of course, is unity. "Now I plead with you, brethren, by the name of our Lord Jesus Christ, that you all speak the same thing, and that there be no divisions among you, but that you be perfectly joined together in the same mind and in the same judgment" (1 Corinthians 1:10).

"I, therefore, the prisoner of the Lord, beseech you to walk worthy of the calling with which you were called, with all lowliness and gentleness, with longsuffering, bearing with one another in love, endeavoring to keep the unity of the Spirit in the bond of peace" (Ephesians 4:1-3).

Identifying the real issue

It is important that we be able to identify the real issues involved in the current division.

THE ISSUE IS NOT

- Opposition to missionary work
- The feeling that orphans should not be provided a home
- Opposition to church cooperation
- Opposition to preaching on radio or television
- How much good is being done

SOME KEY QUESTIONS

- What kind of organization will be used to carry out these activities?
- How can churches cooperate scripturally?
- Can the church have someone else do its work?
- What is the work of the church and what is not the work of the church?

The real issue is related to the kind of arrangement and organization through which these activities should be fulfilled.

Who caused the division?

We need to understand clearly what is involved in the present division among churches of Christ.

Let's imagine for just a moment that someone suggests that, rather than unleavened bread and fruit of the vine, we begin to use cherry pie and milk for the Lord's Supper.

> "Should someone really propose that we eat cherry pie when we observe the Lord's Supper and a division arose over such a suggestion, certainly all of us would understand that the one who suggested and propagated such an idea was the one to bring about the discord, the division. He was the one who was ready to depart from the truth, the pattern given according to scripture.
>
> Why then do we have those who cannot see that these present departures are responsible for the

...bearing with one another in **love**, endeavoring to keep the **unity** of the Spirit in the bond of **peace**.

- Ephesians 4:2-3

present division? Institutional brethren have tried desperately to charge as guilty those who have opposed the innovations they have introduced. They have closed their eyes to the pattern that history has recorded of past departures. It was the group that introduced the instrument in worship that caused the division. It was the group that introduced premillennialism that caused the division. It was the group that introduced the missionary society that caused the division. And it is the group that introduced the present innovations that has caused the present division" (Bob Dickey, *Parkview Persuader*).

Conclusion

We are not trying to encourage division. On the contrary, we want to promote unity among all of God's people. But it must not be a false unity, achieved through compromise of truth. We love peace, but not at any price. The wisdom that is from above is first pure, then peaceable (James 3:17).

The current division among churches of Christ over these issues is not an argument over "methods" used to evangelize the world. It is a division over the basic issues of the organization and mission of the Lord's church.

As we progress in this study, we shall see that the basic problem actually lies in an attitude toward Bible authority.

Questions

1. What is the meaning of the Greek word for "church?"_____
    _____

2. From what are Christians called and into what?_____
    _____
    _____

3. What division does Matthew 10:34-37 say may occur when one decides to become a disciple of Christ?_____
    _____

4. What division does 2 Thessalonians 3:6 tell us is sometimes necessary?
    _____
    _____

5. What division is commanded by God in Romans 16:17? _____
    _____
    _____

6. How would you explain the phrase "the unity of the Spirit?"_____

_____

_____

7. Why is the amount of "good" that something may accomplish not really
    the issue? _____

_____

8. How would you explain the "real issue" to a sincere truth seeker?_____

_____

_____

9. In your view, was the division between Christian churches and churches
    of Christ caused by those who introduced instrumental music or by
    those who opposed it? Explain your answer. _____

_____

_____

10. Why is the wisdom from above, "first pure, then peaceable?" _____

_____

_____

The Need for Bible Authority

In every realm of life, we recognize the need for authority. In the home, the husband is to be the head (Ephesians 5:22-24). At school, there are different levels of authority—the superintendent, the principal, the teachers. In the nation, we have civil government ordained by God with authority to make and enforce laws (Romans 13:1-7).

In each of these areas, problems result when the authority is not heeded or when people set forth their own standards of authority. In religion, this same situation exists. We must have God's authority for all we do. "And whatever you do in word or deed, do all in the name of the Lord Jesus, giving thanks to God the Father through Him" (Colossians 3:17).

> And **whatever** you do in **word** or **deed**, do all in the **name** of the **Lord Jesus**...
>
> - Colossians 3:17

Standards of authority

There are many commonly used standards of authority when it comes to the area of serving God. Some use these false standards without even realizing it.

• Some follow their *conscience* in everything they do religiously.

"Let your conscience be your guide" is their favorite statement. Saul of Tarsus was one who used this standard before he learned the truth. "Then Paul, looking earnestly at the council, said, 'Men and brethren, I have lived in all good conscience before God until this day'" (Acts 23:1). He had killed Christians, thrown many into prison and, in general, "made havoc of the church" (Acts 8:3). He did so with a clear conscience. A conscience must be properly trained or programmed in order to be an accurate guide.

• Others use the standard of *majority opinion.*

If a large enough group believes something to be true and right, surely it is! This overlooks the fact that the majority could be wrong. "Enter by the narrow gate; for wide is the gate and broad is the way that leads to destruction, and there are many who go in by it. Because narrow is the gate and difficult is the way that leads to life, and there are few who find it" (Matthew 7:13-14).

• Many sincere, religious people simply follow the *religion of their parents.*

"If it was good enough for Mom and Dad, it's good enough for me." But, again, this is not an acceptable standard. "And everyone who has left houses or brothers or sisters or father or mother or wife or children or lands, for My name's sake, shall receive a hundredfold, and inherit everlasting life" (Matthew 19:29). In order to properly follow Christ, some will have to choose between the Lord and their families.

The only true standard is the **word of God**, the Bible.

"He who rejects Me, and does not receive My words, has that which judges him—the word that I have spoken will judge him in the last day" (John 12:48).

"All Scripture is given by inspiration of God, and is profitable for doctrine, for reproof, for correction, for instruction in righteousness, that the man of God may be complete, thoroughly equipped for every good work" (2 Timothy 3:16-17).

"But he who looks into the perfect law of liberty and continues in it, and is not a forgetful hearer but a doer of the work, this one will be blessed in what he does" (James 1:25).

"As His divine power has given to us all things that pertain to life and godliness, through the knowledge of Him who called us by glory and virtue" (2 Peter 1:3).

Two kinds of Bible authority

GENERIC

Generic authority is *inclusive*—it includes anything necessary to carry out the command.

The commands to go and to make disciples (teach, KJV) in Matthew 28:19 are generic. "Go therefore and make disciples of all the nations, baptizing them in the name of the Father and of the Son and of the Holy Spirit." They do not specify the manner of going or the method of teaching.

The command in Hebrews 10:25 to assemble (stated negatively—do not forsake) is likewise generic. "Not forsaking the assembling of ourselves together, as is the manner of some, but exhorting one another, and so much the more as you see the Day approaching." It does not say where, what time, etc. It is general in nature.

SPECIFIC

Specific authority is *exclusive*—it excludes everything except what is ordered to carry out the command.

Noah was commanded specifically to build an ark out of gopher wood in Genesis 6:14. "Make yourself an ark of gopher-wood; make rooms in the ark, and cover it inside and outside with pitch." The type of wood was not optional. Because God specified, there were no other acceptable choices.

In partaking of the Lord's Supper, we are told specifically what we are to use as elements in that memorial—bread and cup. "For as often as you eat this bread and drink this cup, you proclaim the Lord's death till He comes" (1 Corinthians 11:26). The cup is referred to as "the fruit of the vine" in Matthew 26:29. God specified those elements and we are not free to change them to something else.

> His divine **power** has given to us **all** things that pertain to **life** and **godliness**...
>
> - 2 Peter 1:3

How Bible authority is established

God communicates His will to us in three ways.

1. *Direct command (or statement)*

   When the Lord issues a direct command (sometimes called a precept), we must obey it to please Him. Baptism is such a command. "And he commanded them to be baptized in the name of the Lord..." (Acts 10:48). This passage does not mention the purpose of baptism, but does teach us that it is a command from God.

   As we have already noticed, commands may be either specific or generic in nature.

Much of the teaching in the Bible is done through the use of simple, easy to understand statements. An example of that is found in Genesis 1:1. "In the beginning God created the heavens and the earth." This does not command us to obey something, nor is it an example that we are expected to follow. But its teaching is clear and concise and we must both teach this truth and defend it whenever and wherever necessary.

Another passage that teaches us through simple statement is Mark 16:16. "He who believes and is baptized will be saved; but he who does not believe will be condemned." This verse does not command us to be baptized and is not an example of anyone being baptized. But it obviously teaches us the importance and necessity of both faith and baptism in the salvation process.

> Brethren, join in **following** my **example**, and **note** those who so **walk**, as you have us for a **pattern**.
>
> - Philippians 3:17

2. *Approved apostolic example*

It is clearly taught in the scriptures that we are to imitate the apostles' example.

"Brethren, join in following my example, and note those who so walk, as you have us for a pattern" (Philippians 3:17).

Notice also Philippians 4:9. "The things which you learned and received and heard and saw in me, these do, and the God of peace will be with you."

Examples must be studied carefully to see if they are incidental (because the same thing is done in another way in a different passage) or binding (because this is the only way we find them being done).

3. *Necessary conclusion* (also called necessary inference, necessary implication or inescapable conclusion)

This refers to those areas of study in which we must understand that something is not specifically stated in the text, but is necessarily implied there. An example of this principle is Hebrews 10:25, quoted earlier. A place for assembling is implied in that generic command. It could be a home, a rented hall, or a "church building" that is owned by the congregation to use in worshiping God. Some place is implied, but not specifically stated.

Notice Romans 3:28: "Therefore we conclude that a man is justified by faith apart from the deeds of the law." Paul draws the conclusion, from what he has just said, that the Old Law has been done away with and we are now saved by faith in Christ and His New Testament, the gospel.

Every time the Bible uses the word, "therefore," the writer is drawing a necessary conclusion based on the things that are stated prior to that point. God expects us to reach those inescapable conclusions and act on, with authority, what has been revealed. There are hundreds of examples of the word "therefore" being used in this way.

Conclusion

The scriptures furnish us completely (2 Timothy 3:16-17). We must not add to nor take from God's word (Revelation 22:18-19). We must not change the gospel in any way (Galatians 1:6-9).

Questions

1. In Colossians 3:17, what does it mean to do something "in the name of the Lord Jesus?"_____

    _____

2. Why is it unsafe to follow one's conscience exclusively?_____

    _____

    _____

3. Why is majority opinion a dangerous standard? _____

    _____

    _____

4. What could possibly be wrong with following the religious traditions of one's parents? _____

    _____

5. What does 2 Timothy 3:16-17 say about God's will?_____

    _____

    _____

6.   What is generic authority? Give an example. _____

_____

_____

_____

7.   What is specific authority? Give an example. _____

_____

_____

_____

8.   How do we decide if a direct command applies to us or not? _____

_____

_____

9.   In Philippians 3:17, what does Paul say about example and pattern?

_____

_____

_____

10. How does a statement of fact teach us to please God? _____

_____

_____

The Silence of the Scriptures

Our plea for scriptural authority in all we do is based on Colossians 3:17—"And whatever you do, in word or deed, do all in the name of the Lord Jesus, giving thanks to the Father through Him."

There are other verses that teach that we must follow the Bible as our guidebook. "If anyone speaks, let him speak as the oracles of God" (1 Peter 4:11). This verse is the basis for the well-known phrase, "we speak where the Bible speaks and we are silent where the Bible is silent."

"Now these things, brethren, I have in a figure transferred to myself and Apollos for your sakes; that in us ye might learn not to go beyond what is written; that no one of you be puffed up for the one against the other" (1 Corinthians 4:6, American Standard Version).

For years, this has been referred to as "book, chapter and verse" preaching and has been the standard call for authority in the Lord's church. But, in recent years, such teaching has become taboo to many and this call for biblical authority for all of our actions has been ridiculed.

Have you ever heard any of these statements about *biblical authority*?

- "We do lots of things without authority."
- "Where does it say we can't?"
- "It doesn't say not to."
- "Where the Bible is silent, we are free to choose."
- "Perhaps we need a new hermeneutic."

Does the silence of the scriptures prohibit certain activities? Or does God's silence allow those activities?

> If anyone **speaks**, let him speak as the **oracles** of **God**.
>
> - 1 Peter 4:11

Then Nadab and Abihu... offered **profane** fire before the Lord, which He had **not commanded** them.

- Leviticus 10:1-2

Bible examples of God's silence

LEVITICUS 10:1-2

"Then Nadab and Abihu, the sons of Aaron, each took his censer and put fire in it, put incense on it, and offered profane fire before the Lord, which He had not commanded them."

Nadab and Abihu offered unauthorized fire before God. They weren't told not to do this; they were simply told what they were supposed to do and then did something else. Their punishment from the Lord was severe and immediate. We are told to learn from such accounts (Romans 15:4).

HEBREWS 1:5

"For to which of the angels did He ever say: 'You are My Son, Today I have begotten You'? And again: 'I will be to Him a Father, and He shall be to Me a Son'?"

This is an argument for the superiority of Christ over the angels based on something God *did not say.*

HEBREWS 7:11-14

"Therefore, if perfection were through the Levitical priesthood (for under it the people received the law), what further need was there that another priest should rise according to the order of Melchizedek, and not be called according to the order of Aaron? ... For it is evident that our Lord arose from Judah, of which tribe Moses spoke nothing concerning priesthood."

Moses did not teach that those from Judah could not be priests; but he told what tribe the priests should come from and silence eliminated all the others, even the tribe from which Christ came. The point of the Hebrew writer is that the law had to be changed so that Christ might be a priest. And he based that conclusion on God's silence.

Basic illustrations

Perhaps a couple of illustrations from everyday life and a couple from the Bible will help us to understand that this is not an unusual communication principle.

- *A search warrant*
  If the police were to enter a home and find evidence that could convict a criminal, they must have authority to be there. They could not argue that a judge hadn't said they could not enter the home.

- *Mail order catalog*
  If you order a tent from a mail order catalog, the people on the other end cannot also send you a lantern, a sleeping bag, an assortment of throw-away utensils, etc. simply because you "didn't tell them not to."

- *Acts 15:23-24*
  "They wrote this letter by them: The apostles, the elders, and the brethren, To the brethren who are of the Gentiles in Antioch, Syria, and Cilicia: Greetings. Since we have heard that some who went out from us have troubled you with words, unsettling your souls, saying, 'You must be circumcised and keep the law'—to whom we gave no such commandment...'"

  Notice that the point is made: we did not teach such a thing, and those who are doing so have no such authority from God. We have been silent about that because God is silent on the subject and to teach it was to add to His word.

- *Lord's Supper elements*
  The Bible clearly teaches that the Lord's Supper is to be observed with bread and fruit of the vine/cup (Matthew 26:26-29). That eliminates everything else! Just imagine how long the Bible would have to be if every other thing that people might want to use had to be specifically mentioned as wrong. It doesn't say not to use pizza and coke, angel food cake and milk, etc. But we know those things are *not* to be substituted.

Some applications

The Bible is silent about the following list of examples, and therefore, there is NO authority to engage in them.

> ...some who went out from us have **troubled** you with words, **unsettling** your souls... to whom we gave **no** such commandment...
>
> - Acts 15:24

- Church sponsored recreation
- Sponsoring church arrangement
- Human institutions doing the work of the church
  - Evangelism—missionary society
  - Edification—"Christian" colleges
  - Benevolence—orphan homes

Other applications

There are numerous applications of this principle that do not necessarily fall under the umbrella of a study of the institutional issues. Perhaps seeing some parallels will help some to understand the lesson more clearly.

For years, those in churches of Christ have worshiped the Lord without instrumental music which accompanies the singing. (We understand, of course, that many have changed their view on this. That is a natural result of abandoning the plea for scriptural authority.) We have consistently and biblically (it is more than mere tradition) taught that God's silence on the use of instruments of music prohibits any instruments from being added to our worship. This is the same principle as the one this lesson is attempting to teach.

Other examples of God's silence include infant baptism, voting on church membership, clergy/laity distinction, and the observance of special holy days. Not one of these commonly practiced activities is found anywhere in God's word. They are not condemned anywhere in the Bible. By the same token, they are not approved anywhere in the Bible. They would only be approved by God if He had included them in His inspired revelation. Therefore, they are all wrong, no matter how widely they are practiced.

Conclusion

Once we begin to practice something not authorized in scripture (either specifically or generically), there is no place to stop. The floodgates have been opened.

There are only two explanations for God's silence on a specific question. God either left it out intentionally or unintentionally. If God intentionally left something out of the Bible, it should be obvious that He did not mean to condone it. If He left it out accidentally, we lose the Bible as a reliable guide.

The real question is: are we going to be satisfied to do just what God tells us to do in the Bible? Or are we going to assume, without biblical evidence, that a particular practice is all right, just because we happen to want it? Let's follow the Bible and respect God's silence.

Questions

1. Define the word "oracle" in 1 Peter 4:11. _____
    _____
    _____

2. What then does it mean to "speak as the oracles of God?" _____
    _____
    _____

3. Why would someone try to justify a particular practice by saying "we do
    lots of things without authority?" _____
    _____
    _____

4. In your own words, explain how Leviticus 10:1-2 illustrates the principle
    of God's silence. _____
    _____
    _____

5. In your own words, explain how Hebrews 1:5 illustrates the principle of
    God's silence. _____
    _____
    _____

6. In your own words, explain how Hebrews 7:11-14 illustrates the
    principle of God's silence. _____
    _____
    _____

7. In your own words, explain how Acts 15:23-24 illustrates the principle of
    God's silence. _____
    _____
    _____

8. God did not say "Do not use pizza and soda for the Lord's Supper."
    Would it be all right to do so because His silence gives us permission?
    Explain your answer._____
    _____
    _____

9. Is instrumental music acceptable to God since He has not specifically prohibited it? Explain your answer. _____

_____

_____

10. Is it safe to assume we can do something God has not revealed in the Bible? If so, what passage of Scripture leads you to that conclusion?

_____

_____

_____

The Church and the Individual

There are many people who do not comprehend the biblical distinction between the corporate body (church) of Christ and the individual Christians who comprise that body.

This is a misconception of God's will that has resulted in much division among the Lord's people. We believe most of our current problems could be solved if we could agree both in theory and practice on this point. Notice this comment from brother Reuel Lemmons.

> "It seems to us that the one and only real principle underlying all the 'issues' of our present time is that of church action versus individual action.
>
> We believe that if this one principle could be resolved, the 'issues'—all of them would disappear. We repeatedly hear the slogan voiced that 'Anything the individual can do the church can do.' We do not believe it. We believe that there are certain things an individual can do, and has an obligation to do, that the church cannot do. The very fact that the Lord provided for an organism called the church is proof positive that it has some function peculiar to itself. If there were no functions peculiar to the church it would be non-essential. There would be no need for it if other capacities could provide all the functions of which it is capable" (*Firm Foundation*, May 3, 1960).

Brother Lemmons and I disagreed on some applications on that principle, but we stood side by side on the principle itself.

Some passages

There are several passages which clearly indicate a distinction between the church and the individual

> For in fact the **body** is not **one** member but **many**.
> - 1 Corinthians 12:14

Christian. Read the verses listed below and notice how they define that distinction.

• *Matthew 18:15-17*

"Moreover if your brother sins against you, go and tell him his fault between you and him alone. If he hears you, you have gained your brother. But if he will not hear you, take with you one or two more, that 'by the mouth of two or three witnesses every word may be established.' And if he refuses to hear them, tell it to the church. But if he refuses even to hear the church, let him be to you like a heathen and a tax collector."

If one individual Christian is the church, he would have "told it to the church" the first time.

• *Acts 5:1-4*

"But a certain man named Ananias, with Sapphira his wife, sold a possession. And he kept back part of the proceeds, his wife also being aware of it, and brought a certain part and laid it at the apostles' feet. But Peter said, 'Ananias, why has Satan filled your heart to lie to the Holy Spirit and keep back part of the price of the land for yourself? While it remained, was it not your own? And after it was sold, was it not in your own control? Why have you conceived this thing in your heart? You have not lied to men, but to God.'"

We clearly see in this passage a difference in the individual's money and that which is given to the Lord's church. Before he brought it, it was his own and he could do with it whatever he desired. But, after he laid it at the apostles' feet (under their authority and control), then it could only be used in a manner authorized for church action.

• *1 Corinthians 12:14*

"For in fact the body is not one member but many."

One cow is not a herd, one sheep is not a flock, one branch is not a vine, and one Christian is not a church.

• *1 Timothy 5:1-16 (especially verses 8, 16)*

"But if anyone does not provide for his own, and especially for those of his own household, he has denied the faith and is worse than an unbeliever" (verse 8).

"If any believing man or woman has widows, let them relieve them, and do not let the church be burdened, that it may relieve those who are really widows" (verse 16).

Described in these verses are two types of widows, those who have family (verse 4) and those who do not (verse 5). "Widows indeed" (those who are really widows, New King James) are unable to take care of themselves and have no one else to provide for them. The church is obligated to provide for them in a permanent way (take them into the number—KJV; put them on the list—NASV; let them be enrolled—ASV). But, individual Christians who have widows are responsible for their care and "do not let the church be burdened." Read verse 16 again very carefully.

Some illustrations

For those who still do not see the scriptural distinction, perhaps some illustrations will help.

I am a member of a family. I am one of several members. What I do, either good or bad, reflects on that family. But, as an individual, I am not a family. A family, by its very nature, requires more than one person. One person is not a family.

I am a citizen of a nation. I am one of several citizens. What I do, either good or bad, reflects on that country. But, as an individual citizen, I am not a nation. A nation, by its very nature, requires more than one citizen. One citizen is not a nation.

As a Christian, I am a member of the family of God. I am a citizen in the kingdom. I am only one of several members/citizens. What I do, good or bad, reflects on that family/kingdom. But, as an individual, I am not the church. The church, by its very nature, requires more than one member. One Christian is not a church.

An important point

It is important for us to realize that an inspired letter can be written and sent to a church and, at the same time, contain instructions for individual Christians to fulfill.

> If any **believing** man or woman has **widows**, let **them** relieve them, and do **not** let the **church** be **burdened**, that it may **relieve** those who are **really** widows.
>
> - 1 Timothy 5:16

Here are a couple of examples.

- The book of 2 Thessalonians was written to the church at Thessalonica (see 1:1). But notice these instructions in 3:11-12. "For we hear that there are some who walk among you in a disorderly manner, not working at all, but are busybodies. Now those who are such we command and exhort through our Lord Jesus Christ that they work with quietness and eat their own bread." Those Christians (as individuals) who were not working and doing their duty were told to repent and change. But it was just for them personally.

- 1 Corinthians was written to the church at Corinth (1:1-2). But in 7:1-3, we have some very personalized instruction for husbands and wives within the church. "Now concerning the things of which you wrote to me: It is good for a man not to touch a woman. Nevertheless, because of sexual immorality, let each man have his own wife, and let each woman have her own husband. Let the husband render to his wife the affection due her, and likewise the wife to her husband." Surely no one would argue that this is "church action" that he is talking about. It was individual instruction contained within a letter addressed to a church.

Two applications

- *Running a business*

The church is taught to raise funds by a freewill offering from the members on the first day of the week (1 Corinthians 16:1-2). An individual can make money any way he wants, as long as it is honest (Ephesians 4:28). But the church is limited to God's plan for giving.

- *Social activities*

Social activities are a duty of the home and family, not the church. Christians in the first century spent much time together socially. But it was always separated from their worship assemblies.

> What! Do you not have **houses** to **eat** and **drink** in? ... But if anyone is hungry, let him **eat** at **home**, lest you come together for **judgment**.
>
> - 1 Corinthians 11:22, 34

The one time we read of an effort to eat together in a social way, as the church, it is condemned and they were told to eat at home (1 Corinthians 11:17-34).

There is no passage in the Bible where social activities, even between Christians, are called "fellowship."

Conclusion

Two of the most often debated passages on this subject are Galatians 6:10 and James 1:27. We will look in detail at each of these verses in future studies. (It is our conviction that both of these verses apply to individual duties before God.)

Failure to understand this scriptural principle has led to serious apostasy. Sincere Christians, who have unwittingly abandoned this principle, are forced to accept all kinds of innovations.

This lack of understanding can lead (and has led) to some rather unbelievable practices among churches of Christ. We now have church widow's homes, church hospitals, church gymnasiums (they sometimes call them "family life centers"), church sponsored softball and basketball teams, choruses and quartet entertainment singing, "fellowship" halls, bake sales, car washes, chili suppers, etc.,—all justified by the argument that there is no distinction between the church and the individual Christian.

Questions

1. "Anything the individual can do, the church can do." Do you believe that? Explain your answer._____

   _____

   _____

2. In your own words, explain how Matthew 18:15-17 makes the distinction between the church and the individual Christian. _____

   _____

   _____

3. In your own words, explain how Acts 5:1-4 makes the distinction between the church and the individual Christian._____

   _____

   _____

4. In your own words, explain how 1 Corinthians 12:14 makes the
    distinction between the church and the individual Christian. _____

    _____

    _____

    _____

5. In your own words, explain how 1 Timothy 5:16 makes the distinction
    between the church and the individual Christian._____

    _____

    _____

    _____

6. Give an example of an individual responsibility found in a letter to a
    church (preferably one not listed in the lesson). _____

    _____

    _____

    _____

7. If the church can do anything the individual can do, is it acceptable for
    the church to raise funds by operating a business? Explain your answer.

    _____

    _____

    _____

    _____

8. Individual Christians can host social activities in their homes to
    whatever extent they want. Can the church do so? Explain your answer.

    _____

    _____

    _____

    _____

9. How can one determine if an instruction is individual or collective?

    _____

    _____

    _____

10. Can you find any verse in which social activities are referred to as
    "fellowship?" _____

    _____

The Work of the Local Church

The work of the Lord's church is spiritual in nature. "These things I write to you, though I hope to come to you shortly; but if I am delayed, I write so that you may know how you ought to conduct yourself in the house of God, which is the church of the living God, the pillar and ground of the truth" (1 Timothy 3:15).

"No man has the right to prostitute the energy, strength, zeal or resources of the church of our Lord to serve human aims or purposes. The church should be kept faithful to the divine mission that was God's purpose from eternity for her to serve" (Roy Cogdill, *Walking by Faith*, page 9).

What the work of the church is *not*

There are many things that modern churches (they aren't really even churches in the biblical usage of that term; we merely use it accommodatively) are involved in activities that have nothing whatsoever to do with the work that God has given His people.

Athletic activities are common today. Churches sponsor softball, basketball and soccer leagues. They build gymnasiums and conduct aerobics classes, exercise classes, provide weight lifting equipment and many other similar endeavors.

Churches today sponsor craft fairs, pie and chili suppers, Thanksgiving, Christmas and Easter banquets to either raise money for the church (God's plan is found in 1 Corinthians 16:1-2) or to simply feed the members (physically, not spiritually).

Churches also are getting more and more involved in entertainment with such things as Christmas and Easter plays, conducted on a very professional level, and these events often draw huge crowds.

> ...I write so that you may know how you ought to **conduct** yourself in the **house** of **God**, which is the **church** of the living God, the **pillar** and **ground** of the **truth**.
>
> - 1 Timothy 3:15

There is a **way** that **seems right** to a **man**, but its **end** is the way of **death**.

- Proverbs 14:12

But do these things please God? Or are they simply examples of human wisdom (Proverbs 14:12) that says, these things bring in large numbers of people and while they are here, let's say something about Jesus? Is the Lord happy with such things? If so, where does the Bible indicate such?

There are also many "service organizations" that can help members of a community in positive ways. Organizations like Alcoholics Anonymous, Narcotics Anonymous, Boy Scouts, Girl Scouts and other similar groups commonly are affiliated with various churches. The issue is not whether such groups help people to live better lives. The issue is whether or not it is the work of the church to sponsor these kinds of civic and social activities. There is simply no scripture that authorizes the Lord's church to engage in these activities.

The standard of what is right and what is wrong is not what our society tells us. It is not what we have gotten used to seeing or doing. The standard of right and wrong is God's word. If it is found in the New Testament, it is right. If it is not found in the Bible, it is wrong.

What the work of the church *is*

The work of a local congregation divides into two categories. Those duties are 1) the worship of God and 2) the saving of souls. Let's study each of these two areas.

THE WORSHIP OF GOD

- *Singing*

    "Speaking to yourselves in psalms and hymns and spiritual songs, singing and making melody in your hearts to the Lord" (Ephesians 5:19; see also Colossians 3:16 and Hebrews 2:12). The early Christians worshiped God in singing praises to His name (Hebrews 13:15). They sang without the accompaniment of musical instruments, blending their voices together to the glory of their Lord.

- *Praying*

  After the establishment of the church, the obedient disciples "...continued steadfastly in the apostles' doctrine...and in prayers" (Acts 2:42). They prayed together (Acts 4:24-31) and those prayers gave them boldness and confidence.

- *The Lord's Supper*

  "Now on the first day of the week, when the disciples came together to break bread, Paul, ready to depart the next day, spoke to them and continued his message until midnight" (Acts 20:7). The first day of the week was the day chosen by the Lord on which the church would remember the sacrifice of Christ through partaking of the memorial service also known as communion (1 Corinthians 10:16). The Lord's church today follows that same pattern.

- *Contribution*

  Another responsibility for Christians, on each Lord's Day, is the giving of their means to carry out the work of the church. "On the first day of the week let each one of you lay something aside, storing up as he may prosper, that there be no collections when I come" (1 Corinthians 16:2). This is the only scriptural way for churches to raise funds.

- *Teaching*

  Acts 20:7 (quoted above) shows us that, when the church assembled for worship, they studied together from the word of God. On this occasion, Paul preached a sermon to them. On other occasions, they read letters from inspired writers (Colossians 4:16). Evangelists, pastors and teachers were put in the church by God to provide for the spiritual growth of disciples (Ephesians 4:11-16).

We could say a lot more about acceptable worship to God, but that is really a subject for a different study. For now, let's spend the rest of this class looking at a second major purpose of the church.

THE SAVING OF SOULS

The second major area of work for the local church is the saving of souls. This sub-divides into four important functions.

- *Evangelism*

  Jesus Christ came into the world to die for those who were lost in sin. "For the Son of Man has come to seek and to save that which was lost" (Luke 19:10). In the Great Commission, Christ instructed His apostles (the men who would begin the church in Acts 2): "Go into all the world and preach the gospel to every creature. He who believes and is baptized will be saved; but he who does not believe will be condemned" (Mark 16:15-16).

• *Edification*

The word "edification" comes from a word which literally means "the act of building or the promotion of spiritual growth and development of character of believers, by teaching or by example, suggesting such spiritual progress as the result of patient labour" (W.E. Vine).

> For the **kingdom** of God is **not eating** and **drinking**, but **righteousness** and **peace** and **joy** in the **Holy Spirit**.
>
> - Romans 14:17

Through study of God's word, prayer, singing and mutual encouragement, Christians are to help one another "grow in the grace and knowledge of our Lord and Savior Jesus Christ" (2 Peter 3:18). One of the stated reasons for our worship assemblies is "to stir up love and good works" (Hebrews 10:24-25).

• *Benevolence*

As the church carried out its work, they occasionally had situations in which Christians faced financial difficulties. They always helped one another as they had the ability (Acts 2:44-45; 4:34-35; 6:1-4; 11:27-30; Romans 15:25-31; 1 Corinthians 16:1-3; 2 Corinthians 8 and 9; 1 Timothy 5:1-16). In every instance, the benevolence of the local church was limited to needy saints. We will discuss this subject in more detail in Lesson 10.

• *Church discipline*

On occasion, those who obey the Lord become unfaithful. Church discipline is an attempt to restore and save those who have returned to the world. "But we command you, brethren, in the name of our Lord Jesus Christ, that you withdraw from every brother who walks disorderly and not according to the tradition which he received from us" (2 Thessalonians 3:6). Other passages which refer to this process are 1 Corinthians 5, Romans 16:17-18, Titus 3:10-11, and James 5:19-20.

Conclusion

"It should be remembered that as a divine institution the church has a divine mission. It is neither political, nor social, but altogether spiritual in its design. Its concern is not the entertainment of people but the saving of souls" (Roy Cogdill, *The New Testament Church*, page 24).

The work of the local church is wholly spiritual in its nature (Romans 14:17). Let no one attempt to alter what God has ordained His church to perform as her divine mission.

Questions

1. Explain this phrase: "that you may know how you ought to conduct yourself in the house of God."_____

   _____

   _____

2. Do you know of any New Testament verses that authorize the church to sponsor athletic teams, exercise classes or craft fairs? _____

3. How is the church authorized to raise funds? _____

   _____

   _____

4. What are the two primary functions of the church?_____

   _____

5. Define evangelism._____

   _____

6. Define edification. _____

   _____

7. Define benevolence._____

   _____

8. What is meant by the phrase "church discipline?"_____

   _____

   _____

9. Does the church have any political duties? Explain your answer. _____

    _____

    _____

10. What information about the work of the church is found in Romans 14:17?

    _____

    _____

    _____

Scriptural Church Cooperation

The charge is often made against non-institutional brethren that we are "anti-cooperation." The impression is created that such churches are against churches cooperating in preaching the gospel. This impression is false. The opposition is not to church cooperation, but to what we consider, according to the Bible, to be unscriptural church cooperation.

We must have Bible authority for all that we do (Colossians 3:17) and church cooperation is no exception. The Bible reveals how churches may cooperate scripturally. This is the pattern we must follow if we seek to have the Lord's approval.

"To deny that churches in New Testament times cooperated would be foolish indeed since Inspiration affirms such. The pattern for such cooperation is as clear as is the pattern for proper worship in song or as to who is a fit candidate for baptism. Churches cooperated in both benevolence and evangelism. However, it must be carefully observed at the outset that such cooperation was not of the sort where there was an intermediate institution, not a pooling of resources between the local church and the work to be done, nor is there any instance in the New Testament of several churches sending to one church which had assumed to do a work to which all shared equal obligation" (Dee Bowman, "Scriptural Cooperation VS. the Sponsoring Church," *Searching the Scriptures* magazine, August, 1978).

We will have more to say about the sponsoring church arrangement in the next study. This lesson is focused on how churches can cooperate scripturally.

> And **whatever** you do in **word** or **deed**, do all in the **name** of the **Lord Jesus**...
>
> - Colossians 3:17

...To all the **saints** in Christ Jesus who are in Philippi, with the **bishops** and **deacons**:

- Philippians 1:1

The pattern for cooperation

1. *No other organization than the church*

In the first century, Christians were organized into local churches in various localities and those churches did the Lord's work in their area. Each congregation, when mature, was organized with elders, deacons and saints (Philippians 1:1). There were no other organizations at all.

- There was no missionary society through which the local church could evangelize.

- There was no organization like a Bible college through which the local church could edify itself and train preachers and teachers.

- There were no group homes through which the needy (orphans, widows, etc.) could be cared for as part of the church's work of benevolence.

Whether or not these organizations (they are sometimes called para-church organizations) have the right to exist if they are supported privately, rather than from the church treasury, is a subject for a different study. Here, it is simply pointed out that the local church, in the first century, did its work personally and not through such institutions.

In Bible times, there was no organization smaller (like the denominational Sunday school organization) or larger (like the denominational district or the sponsoring church arrangement) than the local church.

2. *Independent action of churches*

Churches in the first century worked together to evangelize the world. They did so by each local church doing its part, according to its ability and opportunities, to reach the lost. There was no centralized headquarters which coordinated those efforts. Each group did what it could to reach common goals.

That is not to say that there was no communication or cooperation between groups. But one group was not required to "check with" another group before acting. No one had the right to declare a "mission area" as being exclusively their work and that everyone else should stay away.

Obviously, if one group is reaching out to a segment of society or a certain geographical area, it would be wise for another group to concentrate its efforts elsewhere. And that kind of cooperation is wise.

In this work, it is possible for churches to work together in supporting a preacher at a particular location to preach. Paul stated that, in his work at Corinth, several churches helped to finance that effort. "I robbed other churches (note the plural, rh), taking wages of them to minister to you" (2 Corinthians 11:8). But they did not pool their money through a sponsoring church and then have it sent to Paul. Each supporting church sent what they could to the apostle.

In his evangelistic work in Thessalonica, Paul was supported financially by one church, Philippi. "Nevertheless you have done well that you have shared in my distress. Now you Philippians know also that in the beginning of the gospel, when I departed from Macedonia, no church shared with me concerning giving and receiving but you only. For even in Thessalonica you sent aid once and again for my necessities. Not that I seek the gift, but I seek the fruit that abounds to your account. Indeed I have all and abound. I am full, having received from Epaphroditus the things which were sent from you, a sweet-smelling aroma, an acceptable sacrifice, well pleasing to God" (Philippians 4:14-18).

The congregations, while working (cooperating) to achieve the same goal, helped independently of one another. No one told another church to give, how much to give, that they could not give, etc.

Now you **Philippians** know also that in the beginning of the **gospel**, when I departed from Macedonia, no **church shared** with me concerning **giving** and **receiving** but you only.

- Philippians 4:15

It was concurrent cooperation, with each group (church) working separately toward a common goal. It was not joint cooperation in which churches were joined together structurally or financially.

It is important to realize that, in financially supporting gospel preachers, each congregation sent their support directly to the preacher, not to another church to then give to a preacher (Philippians 4:15). As we noted previously, other churches (plural) supported Paul while he preached in Corinth. They did not send the money to the Corinthian treasurer to compile together and then give to Paul. They all supported Paul directly, but not jointly into one common fund.

3. *Autonomy of each local church*

Each local church had elders (Acts 14:23; appointed after a period of time, not right away). Those elders made decisions for that local church and how it would spend its money. They were not answerable to any other group of elders. They simply cared for the flock which was "among them" (Acts 20:28; 1 Peter 5:1-2).

Here is the same teaching in chart form with some examples of violations of the divine pattern added:

Scriptural	Unscriptural
No other organization than the local church	Human organizations which do the work of the Lord's church
Independent action of each church	Joint action of congregations
Autonomy of each local church	Sponsoring church arrangement

We will have more to say about local church autonomy in Lesson 9.

Scriptural cooperation

There are many ways in which local congregations can and should cooperate with one another in accomplishing the Lord's work. Here are just a few examples:

• Many churches can cooperate in supporting a gospel preacher in an area where the church is weak, small or even non-existent. A look at the preacher support letters on most church bulletin boards will show that "conservative" churches cooperate with many other congregations in this way.

• Churches should try, as much as possible, not to conflict in the scheduling of activities, such as Vacation Bible School, gospel meetings, lectureships, etc.

• Churches should share ideas and talk about things that have been helpful in their local work. Preachers and elders could get together occasionally and talk about the Lord's work and, under no obligation to follow another's example, share with each other what they have done successfully.

Conclusion

Let it be understood that, while we do not oppose any scriptural church cooperation, we do oppose the sponsoring church arrangement for cooperation.

"In New Testament times, the basis for any cooperation was need. When the need no longer existed neither did the cooperation. The sponsoring church creates a permanent need. In doing so, it violates the New Testament order. Furthermore, none of the New Testament examples show any church giving anything to another church for accomplishing a work to which all churches were equally related. The command to evangelize the world is the work of every church and there is NO example in the New Testament of one church contributing funds to help another church evangelize the world, for all churches are equally obligatory to such an assignment" (Dee Bowman, ibid.).

The Bible teaches concurrent cooperation (independent action of churches cooperating to achieve the same end result) but it does not teach joint cooperation (the pooling of structure or funds).

Questions

1. True or False? Conservative churches are opposed to any form of church cooperation. Explain your answer._____

   _____

   _____

2. How are we going to be able to determine how churches can cooperate scripturally? _____

   _____

   _____

3. How did the New Testament church train preachers? _____

   _____

   _____

4. Can you show from the New Testament any examples of a larger organization than a local church? If so, what is it?_____

   _____

5. Paul states that, while he was preaching in Corinth, he did not take a salary from the church. How does he say he got paid? _____

    _____

    _____

6. How many churches supported Paul financially while he preached in Thessalonica? _____

7. Does the church where you worship help to support gospel preachers in other areas of the world? (Check the bulletin board or ask someone who would know.) If so, list a couple of the preacher's names and where they preach._____

    _____

    _____

8. What would be some advantages of elders talking to other elders about their respective work?_____

    _____

    _____

9. What would be some disadvantages or concerns about elders getting together and talking about ideas?_____

    _____

    _____

10. Give some other examples of ways you believe congregations can scripturally cooperate._____

    _____

    _____

    _____

The Sponsoring Church Arrangement

One of the major problem areas in this study revolves around the concept of the "sponsoring church" arrangement. In this arrangement, one church becomes the headquarters through which other churches channel and pool their funds. The sponsoring church then appropriates the money to various needs, such as a preacher in a needy area or a large scale program, like a nationwide radio program. (The Herald of Truth radio program, with the Highland church in Abilene, Texas as the sponsoring church was the catalyst for division in the 1950's and 1960's.)

The biblical pattern is for a church (or several churches) to send support directly to an evangelist. The problem arises when a church decides to take on a work which it cannot afford, such as a national or worldwide radio or television program. It begins to solicit funds from other churches to support this work and denounces those who do not believe in such a financial arrangement as "anti-cooperation."

Sometimes this arrangement is set up as a practical way to handle a preacher's outside support. Rather than having numerous congregations each sending their support directly to a preacher, each one sends the funds to the preacher's "sponsoring congregation," which then forwards the total into a bank account for the preacher.

sponsoring church: a congregation that operates as a headquarters through which other churches channel and pool their funds

What is cooperation?

When we speak of church cooperation, we are discussing how churches may scripturally work together to accomplish the Lord's work. The word, cooperation, means working together. A husband and wife cooperate in the rearing of their children. Workers on the job cooperate to accomplish the work of the business. Players on a team cooperate, or work together, to achieve the victory. Soldiers in the armed forces work together to defeat the enemy. Churches cooperate with each other in defeating the devil and saving as many souls as possible.

But we must make certain that our cooperation is according to God's pattern and is not merely another example of human wisdom that makes sense to us, but sets aside God's eternal plan and purpose for His church.

Two kinds of cooperation

It is important that we recognize that there are two different kinds of church cooperation. One is scriptural; the other is not.

The first kind of cooperation is called *joint cooperation*. This type of cooperation includes a pooling of funds, combining the money contributed by two or more local churches and placing the control of those funds under a single church's eldership. It generally also involves an organization in place to manage those funds, often the eldership of the receiving church, making decisions about how those funds are to be used and/or distributed. The contributing congregations have little or no say in any decisions about the money, once they decide to contribute it to the cooperative effort.

Joint cooperation is typified by the sponsoring church arrangement. In this setup, a congregation decides to start a work which it cannot fully support alone. It may be the full support for a preacher. It may be a radio or television program to reach a vast audience with the gospel. But the host church decides to accept the responsibility for overseeing this work and agrees to be the central agency for collecting funds from other churches and for providing the day to day management of that work. This structure of cooperation is not found in the New Testament.

The other type of cooperation could be called *independent but concurrent cooperation*. In this

> So also the Lord directed those who **proclaim** the **gospel** to get their **living** from the **gospel**.
>
> - 1 Corinthians 9:14

method of cooperation, each autonomous congregation (we'll study more about autonomy in Lesson 9) does the work that God has designed the local church to do, in evangelizing the lost and edifying the saved.

Each church works toward the common goal of saving as many souls as possible for the Lord. Each church works under the local authority of its Holy Spirit ordained elders (Acts 20:28). Each church limits itself to doing what it can do, given the authority of the scriptures and the financial resources provided through the freewill contributions of its members. The elders do not dictate to any other church, nor do they accept oversight of their work by any other eldership. They join hundreds of other churches around their immediate area and around the world in doing the Lord's work of saving the lost. Together they may help to financially support gospel preachers to work in foreign fields and weak areas of their own country.

They simply do the work God has assigned them to do and encourage churches in other places to do exactly the same. They do not pool their funds or combine their organizations to form something foreign to the New Testament. They do the Lord's work in the Lord's way, according to their ability and opportunity.

God's plan

What God has authorized in the New Testament is for the sending church to give the money directly to the gospel preacher. That is what is taught in passages like 1 Corinthians 9:14-17 and Philippians 4:15-17. It looks like this:

In some instances, numerous churches contribute to the support of one preacher (2 Corinthians 11:8) as pictured below:

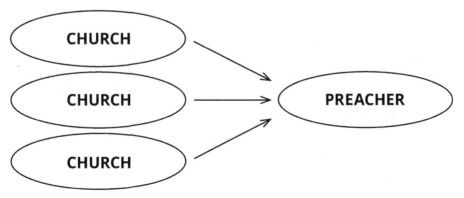

Man's plan

In the sponsoring church arrangement, the money from numerous congregations is sent to one central church which then supports the preacher. This plan would be diagrammed as follows:

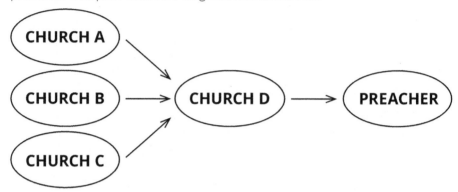

There are no verses from the New Testament that can be found to justify this plan.

Limits to the work of a local church

One of the things that we must all understand is that the work of a local church is limited to its ability and its opportunity. (The word responsibility is formed by combining the ideas of response to ability.) A church is not responsible to do something beyond its ability to do. While the Lord expects each local church to do all it can, and many of us could be doing much more than we are, He never expects any local church to do more than it can.

If each local church will do all it can, there will be no need to form extra-biblical organizations to try to "improve" on God's plan. The problem is that, so often, we fall short of being what we ought to be and doing what we ought to do, and some people (good hearted people) want to try to accomplish more.

But, unfortunately, such people often come up with a plan that changes God's pattern given in the New Testament. We can never improve on God's plan and design for the church.

A huge problem

One of the biggest problems with the sponsoring church arrangement is that it puts an eldership over the work of more than one church. Is there a scripture authorizing that? If so, what would it be? A sponsoring church eldership is actually overseeing the work of many congregations, by overseeing and controlling the money contributed by those many congregations.

And, as people have tried to point out for years, if a single eldership can oversee the work of more than one congregation, what would be wrong with that eldership overseeing the work of all the congregations? What is wrong with it, of course, is that there is no scripture which teaches it, therefore it is sinful. Most people can see the truth in that, when this extreme situation is described. But, there is also no scripture for a single eldership to oversee the work of even two congregations, only one.

It is important to remember that one of the first major apostasies for the church was in the realm of church organization. The final result was the Roman Catholic Church.

What about Acts 11:27-30?

Acts 11:27-30 has often been cited as scriptural proof for the sponsoring church arrangement. It reads like this: "And in those days prophets came from Jerusalem to Antioch. Then one of them, named Agabus, stood up and showed by the Spirit that there was going to be a great famine throughout all the world, which also happened in the days of Claudius Caesar. Then the disciples, each according to his ability, determined to send relief to the brethren dwelling in Judea. This they also did, and sent it to the elders by the hands of Barnabas and Saul."

This is not an example of a sponsoring church. It is an example of some needy churches (in Judea) that could not care for their own members being helped by Christians from other areas. Evangelism and benevolence are not the same thing. There is one pattern for evangelism and another for benevolence.

Then the **disciples**, each according to his **ability**, determined to send **relief** to the **brethren** dwelling in Judea. This they also did, and sent it to the **elders** by the hands of Barnabas and Saul.

- Acts 11:29-30

The difference between Acts 11:27-30 and the sponsoring church arrangement is substantial. In Acts 11, the churches did not decide to be poor. It just happened, as events beyond their control unfolded.

However, in the modern situation, the "sponsoring church" takes it upon itself to do a great work for the brotherhood, finds itself unable to financially support this "bigger than a single church" project, and then expects other churches to bail it out financially. Sponsoring churches are not needy churches. They have simply overstretched their ability to support what they want to do.

Conclusion

This study is a matter of either following God's arrangement of local churches, acting autonomously and independently, yet concurrently, to do the Lord's work or man's plan of pooling funds and forming a new structure, the sponsoring church, which oversees, distributes funds and controls at least part of the work of the contributing churches.

Questions

1. What does "cooperation" mean? _____

    _____

    _____

2. What is meant by "joint" cooperation? _____

    _____

    _____

3. What is meant by "independent, but concurrent" cooperation? _____

    _____

    _____

4. What is a sponsoring church? _____

    _____

    _____

5. What is the pattern for cooperation in supporting an evangelist? _____

    _____

    _____

6. Can you find a passage which teaches that an eldership may oversee more than one church and its work on a sponsoring church level? If so, what is it? _____

7. What is the limiting factor in any work assigned to the Lord's church? Explain your answer._____

    _____

    _____

8. What major religious denomination resulted from gradual changes in God's New Testament pattern for church organization? _____

    _____

9. Does Acts 11:27-30 authorize a sponsoring church arrangement? Explain your answer._____

    _____

    _____

    _____

Institutionalism

"If the church of the Lord is sufficient to accomplish what the Lord intended for it to do, it is competent, adequate, and no other organization or arrangement is permitted, much less needed. Any effort made by man to add to or improve upon the Lord's arrangement for the accomplishment of His purpose through His church indicates dissatisfaction with God's ways" (Roy Cogdill, *Walking by Faith*, page 10).

What is the church?

When we speak of the church, we refer to the body of Jesus Christ, purchased with His shed blood (Acts 20:28). In its universal sense, it is the collective number of all saved people. It is undenominational in its nature, is singular in its design, and it has only one head, Jesus Himself.

"And I also say to you that you are Peter, and on this rock *(Peter's confession of Jesus as the Christ, rh)* I will build My church, and the gates of Hades shall not prevail against it" (Matthew 16:18).

"And He *(God, rh)* put all things under His *(Christ's, rh)* feet, and gave Him to be head over all things to the church, which is His body, the fullness of Him who fills all in all" (Ephesians 1:22-23).

"There is one body..." (Ephesians 4:4). This is the universal church, composed of all saved people.

The church is known in the Bible by a variety of terms. Some of them are the kingdom (Colossians 1:13), the household of faith (Galatians 6:10), the flock of God (1 Peter 5:2), the bride of Christ (Ephesians 5:22-23), the pillar and ground of the truth (1 Timothy 3:15).

He has **delivered** us from the power of darkness and **conveyed** us into the **kingdom** of the **Son** of His **love**.

- Colossians 1:13

What is an institution?

"To 'institute' is 'to set up or establish.' The word 'institution' as we shall use it in this study means; 'An organization or establishment instituted for some public, educational, or charitable purpose' (Webster). Whether an institution is divine or human depends upon whether it was established by God or man" (Eugene Britnell, "Church Supported Human Institutions," *Searching the Scriptures* magazine, August, 1978).

The church is one of only three divinely ordained institutions in the world. They are the home, civil government and the church. All others are human institutions.

The church is a divine institution. It was designed in the mind of God, as part of His plan for human redemption, before the world even began. "...to the intent that now the manifold wisdom of God might be made known by the church to the principalities and powers in the heavenly places, according to the eternal purpose which He accomplished in Christ Jesus our Lord" (Ephesians 3:10-11). Notice here that the church was in God's eternal purpose.

The local church

Each congregation is to be organized, according to the New Testament pattern, with elders, deacons and saints (Philippians 1:1).

The elders are the spiritual leaders or rulers of a local church. They are also called bishops, presbyters, overseers, shepherds or pastors. They must meet the qualifications set forth by God in 1 Timothy 3:1-7 and Titus 1:5-9. They are in charge of the spiritual oversight of the members who place themselves under that oversight and they are to watch out for the souls of those members (1 Thessalonians 5:12-13; Hebrews 13:17).

The deacons are servants, specially qualified servants (1 Timothy 3:8-13) who serve the congregation under

And we urge you, brethren, to **recognize** those who **labor** among you, and are **over** you in the **Lord** and **admonish** you...

- 1 Thessalonians 5:12

the oversight of, and as directed by, the elders. They may be put in charge of whatever work the elders determine needs to be done, according to the various abilities that each man possesses.

Saints are simply Christians. We might refer to them as "the members of the church." The word, saint, means sanctified or holy one. It speaks of the godly, holy life that disciples of Jesus Christ are taught to live, in the New Testament.

(Evangelists, by the way, are not "church officers." They are simply Christians, or saints, who work under the oversight of the elders and who spend their time preaching and teaching the word of God.)

There is no other functioning unit in the Lord's plan than the local church.

The all-sufficiency of the church

Some important questions need to be asked at this point in our study. Is the church, as designed by God and described on the pages of the New Testament, sufficient to do the work that God intended for it to do? Or does the church need the help of human institutions? Did God plan and organize the church so it can accomplish God's will? Or does God's plan fall short?

Human institutions, supported by the Lord's money, represent the view that the church is not sufficient to carry out the mission that God designed it to accomplish.

While those who endorse such organizations would not say so out loud, they are really claiming that the church cannot do the work that God intended it to do without the existence of these additional human institutions.

In contrast to the church as a divine institution, we are seeking to examine the place of human institutions in the plan of God. Was it ever God's purpose for His church to carry out part or all of its work through human organizations?

The answer, of course, is no.

> For those who have served well as **deacons** obtain for themselves a **good standing** and great **boldness** in the **faith** which is in Christ Jesus.
>
> - 1 Timothy 3:13

God's plan is simple; it looks like this: **Man's plan** looks like this:

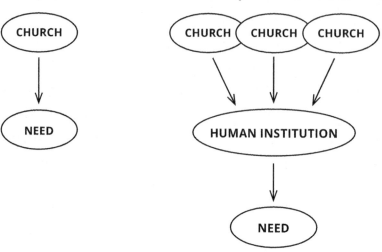

Examples of human institutions

There are several examples of human institutions that brethren have created over the years that, every single time, have brought division and heartache to the body of Christ.

In the field of evangelism, one of the more popular human institutions is the **missionary society**.

In the area of edification, the church supported **Bible college** is often used to "help the church" train preachers or educate brethren.

In the realm of benevolence, human institutions would include **orphan homes**, **nursing homes** and **hospitals**.

Again, be honest and ask yourself, can the church do the work God has assigned it to do in the areas of evangelism, edification and benevolence without the help of any human institution? Is the church all sufficient to do God's work?

A missing link?

"Those who feel that the church is related to and must work through human institutions are trying to supply a 'missing link' in God's plan. Any Bible student should know that there is no organization or arrangement in the New Testament by which churches are tied together or which can activate the church on a county, state, regional, national or universal level. So men have built such organizations and declared that without them churches, at least many of them, cannot work effectively" (Eugene Britnell, ibid.).

Purchasing a service or making a donation?

The local church has an obligation to care for one who is "really a widow," and meets the scriptural qualifications found in 1 Timothy 5:9-11. This could be done by paying her expenses at a Baptist, Methodist, or Lutheran nursing home. The church is merely purchasing a service, as it would do in buying class material from a bookstore, grape juice for communion from a grocery store, or a projector for teaching from an office supply business. But, of course, it does not follow that the church can make regular contributions to a Methodist nursing home, a religious bookstore, a grocery store, or an office supply store. One is scriptural; the other is not.

Conclusion

"May we plead that the church be the church and do the work of the church by the simple and sufficient operation of the arrangement God has given— the congregation. There is no authority in the scriptures for the church contributing to or working through human institutions" (Britnell, ibid.).

Questions

1. What is the church (Matthew 16:18)?_____
    _____
    _____

2. What is a human institution?_____
    _____
    _____

3. Name three divinely ordained institutions.
    _____
    _____
    _____

4. How does Ephesians 3:10-11 describe the church? _____
    _____
    _____

5. How is a local church to be organized (Philippians 1:1)?_____
    _____
    _____

6. How do human institutions reflect upon the all-sufficiency of the Lord's church?_____

_____

_____

7. Give an example of a human institution in each of these areas of work:
Evangelism _____
Edification_____
Benevolence _____

8. In your opinion, is the human institution a "missing link" which will help the church to do its work more effectively? Explain your answer.

_____

_____

_____

9. Could the church care for a "widow indeed" (1 Timothy 5) by paying her bills at a Methodist rest home? Explain your answer. _____

_____

_____

_____

10. Could the same church then make regular donations to that home? Explain your answer._____

_____

_____

_____

Local Church Autonomy

The autonomy of the local church is one of the safeguards that God has given His people to prevent us from digressing into apostasy. This study will highlight what the Bible says about the issue of autonomy.

What is autonomy?

By the term, autonomy, we simply mean self-rule, independence or self-government. It is the scriptural plan that each congregation has its own biblically prescribed government and that no outside pressure is to be exerted on the decisions made by the leadership of each church. They might be influenced by the positive example and faithfulness of others. But no one else has the authority to dictate to a local church what they must do.

autonomy: self-rule, independence or self-government

Each local church is subject to only one higher authority, Jesus Christ Himself. He is the head of the church and the only One who can tell the church what to do. "Then Jesus came and spoke to them, saying, 'All authority has been given to Me in heaven and on earth'" (Matthew 28:18). There is but one level of authority above a congregation, the Head, Jesus Christ. There is not a head in heaven and a head on earth. There is only Jesus.

The local church

The congregation is the only functioning organization of the Lord's people.

"Paul and Timothy, servants of Jesus Christ, To all the saints in Christ Jesus who are in Philippi, with the bishops and deacons" (Philippians 1:1). There is no

> So when they had appointed **elders** in **every church**, and prayed with fasting, they **commended** them to the **Lord** in whom they had **believed**.
>
> - Acts 14:23

other congregational structure that pleases the Lord. The bishops (also called elders in other passages) are the spiritual leaders of the church. The deacons are trustworthy, reliable servants who meet the needs of the elders and the other church members. The saints are the Christians, or disciples of Christ.

The elders are men who meet certain scriptural qualifications, as set forth in 1 Timothy 3:1-7 and Titus 1:5-9. God's plan is for each church to have a qualified eldership that oversees the flock, directs its work and protects the church from the sinful work of false teachers.

In New Testament times, elders were appointed fairly quickly after the congregation was established. The first mention of elders serving a local church is found in Acts 11:30. At the conclusion of Paul's first preaching tour, he returned to many of the churches he had planted earlier on the journey and appointed elders (Acts 14:23). Notice that the passage says that they were appointed "in every church." Those that did not yet have elders serving were to be working to that end, because they were said to be "lacking" what God desired for them.

Limits to elders' authority

According to God's word, an eldership only has the authority to oversee one congregation, never more than one.

"Shepherd the flock of God which is among you, serving as overseers, not by constraint but willingly, not for dishonest gain but eagerly; nor as being lords over those entrusted to you, but being examples to the flock" (1 Peter 5:2). Did you note the phrase, "which is among you?" That is the limiting phrase to the authority of elders.

"Therefore take heed to yourselves and to all the flock, among which the Holy Spirit has made you overseers, to shepherd the church of God, which He purchased with His own blood" (Acts 20:28). This was a different eldership and a different

New Testament writer and, yet, the message is consistent. They were to watch "the flock, among which" they labored.

"And we urge you, brethren, to recognize those who labor among you, and are over you in the Lord and admonish you, and to esteem them very highly in love for their work's sake. Be at peace among yourselves" (1 Thessalonians 5:12). This passage is written to the church (the last two passages were directed to the elders). It says, again, that the ones to be esteemed and highly appreciated were those who "labor among you."

A second limitation to the authority of elders is that they must rule within the parameters of God's word. They must not "go beyond what is written" (1 Corinthians 4:6, American Standard Version).

Elders, therefore, exercise their authority in the realm of judgment decisions that must be made in each local church. They do not have law giving authority, but must be content to remain inside "the doctrine of Christ" (2 John 9-11). If they wander outside of the Bible, they do "not have God."

> Whoever **transgresses** and does not **abide** in the **doctrine** of **Christ** does not have **God**.
>
> - 2 John 9

Areas of judgment	Areas of truth/ doctrine
An eldership can decide who will work with the church as a preacher, who will hold gospel meetings, what time services will be, how quickly to move in a church discipline situation, who will be used to conduct worship services, and many other decisions that are in the realm of personal judgment. Someone must make such decisions and God has given that authority to the elders.	An eldership does not have the authority to decide how often the Lord's Supper should be observed, whether or not the church will use instruments of music, if the church will build a gymnasium for the amusement of the members, whether there will be public prayers in worship. These kinds of "doctrinal" decisions are a matter of revelation from God, not judgments in areas of opinion that do not matter.

Elders are not law givers. There is only one of those (James 4:12) and His name is Jesus. The elders are simply those who are to spiritually lead others in following God's laws.

Some applications

Modern denominationalism, with its centralization of power and authority, has developed many different forms of "church government." There are hundreds of different man-made denominations and each one comes up with its own ideas about how that group will be organized. In the New Testament, there was nothing smaller or larger than the local church. There was no separate Sunday school with its own officers and collections and work. There were no "super-organizations," like regions, districts, synods, councils, or denominational headquarters. The purpose of these structures is to dictate policy to individual congregations, to make decisions somewhere else that ought to be decided locally. One of the sinful characteristics of denominationalism is its unscriptural organizational structures.	**The sponsoring church arrangement**, while popular among institutional churches (as we studied in Lesson Seven), is another example of man's wisdom being preferred by some over God's simple plan for congregational autonomy. The sponsoring church concept involves many congregations (as many as the sponsoring church can convince to do so) pooling their resources and funds to do a "bigger work" than any one local church could do. The smaller churches send their money to one big church, which places that sponsoring church eldership over many churches, rather than over just one, as God's word teaches. Remember that the responsibility of one congregation is limited by ability and opportunity. The problem comes when a congregation decides to take upon itself a work which it does not have the ability to support.

A brotherhood work?

It is very tempting for brethren to want to do a "great work" for the whole brotherhood. Doing big things in a big way has a certain appeal. This desire can lead some people into schemes that have little or nothing to do with God's plan for the church.

Simply put, there is no such thing as a "brotherhood work." There is no functioning unit in God's word any larger than the local church. Those who propose to do some huge work of national or international significance need to be content with doing God's work in God's way.

The Bible teaches one duty of a Christian in relation to "the brotherhood." It is found in 1 Peter 2:17. "Honor all people. Love the brotherhood. Fear God.

Honor the king." That's it—just love the brotherhood. But do not assume to do a work that violates the autonomy of the local church in an attempt to do something bigger than God wants.

"In support of their brotherhood projects innovators fail to see that there is a clear distinction between the church in its local and universal sense. They say, 'If the local congregation can scripturally do this work, then it is something that any or all congregations could collectively do as the one church.' This error is basic and fundamental to the departures of institutionalism. It is a serious move indeed when the nature of the church is misrepresented" (Bob Dickey, *Parkview Persuader*).

The universal and local church

The sponsoring church arrangement is an effort to activate the church in its universal sense. It is important for us to recognize and understand the scriptural distinction between a local church and the church universal. The following chart should help to clarify some of those differences.

Church Universal	Church Local
Matthew 16:18; Ephesians 1:22-23; Ephesians 5:23-27; Hebrews 12:23	Romans 16:16; 1 Corinthians 1:2; Colossians 4:15-16; Revelation 2 and 3
There is only one	There are many
One is added to it (Acts 2:47)	One must join (Acts 9:26)
Began on Pentecost (Acts 2)	May begin at any time
Saint dies – still in it	Saint dies – no longer a part
No earthly organization	Earthly organization (Philippians 1:1)
Cannot pool funds	Must pool funds (1 Corinthians 16:1-2)
Has no work	Must work

"The New Testament scriptures are completely silent as to any universal function of the church and as to any universal organization through which such a function might be performed. If God had intended for the church universal to perform any function upon the earth is it not self evident that He would have been wise enough to give it a medium or organization through which to perform that function? The necessary conclusion then is that since God has given the church only a local organization – the congregation – He intended for its function and work to be executed through the local church as a medium. When we depart from such a medium in trying to serve God in the church, we leave God's plan and become disobedient and irreverent" (Roy Cogdill, *Walking by Faith*, page 86).

Conclusion

A local church, with its God-given organization, has no outside accountability, except to the Lord. A local church does not have to answer to anyone else, including another eldership, editors of magazines, a college run by brethren, other churches, other preachers, or any other bullies who want to run everyone else's business.

Questions

1. What is autonomy? _____
   _____
   _____

2. What is the only level of authority higher than the local church? _____
   _____
   _____

3. Who are the spiritual leaders of a local church? Give scriptures to prove your answer. _____
   _____
   _____

4. What are some examples of decisions elders can make? _____
   _____
   _____
   _____

5. What are some examples of decisions elders cannot make? _____
   _____
   _____
   _____

6. How many churches can an eldership oversee? List scriptures to prove your answer. _____
   _____
   _____

7. Give an example of an organization larger than the local church. _____
   _____
   _____

LESSON 9 Local Church Autonomy 61

8. What is a Christian's duty to the brotherhood? _____
   _____
   _____

9. List at least two differences in the universal church and the local
   church. _____
   _____
   _____

10. Can you think of any verse that assigns a specific "work" to the universal
    church? _____
   _____
   _____

The Extent of Benevolence

Benevolence is always an emotional subject to discuss. Decisions have to made about who needs help, how much should be given (if any), how long such help should continue, etc. Many of these things are matters of judgment and, of course, opinions vary from person to person. (That is one of the advantages of being in a church with elders and deacons, chosen and appointed by the congregation to deal with such matters.)

It is our conviction that benevolence is a "secondary" work of the church. The church is a spiritual organization with spiritual work - to praise God and to save souls. But, on occasion, those souls get into financial difficulties and need some assistance. What does the Bible teach about our obligations to help them?

First of all, we understand that those who are lazy and unwilling to work do not deserve help from anyone. "For even when we were with you, we commanded you this: If anyone will not work, neither shall he eat. For we hear that there are some who walk among you in a disorderly manner, not working at all, but are busybodies. Now those who are such we command and exhort through our Lord Jesus Christ that they work in quietness and eat their own bread" (2 Thessalonians 3:10-12). For those who simply will not work, God says "Get a job!"

Others may be guilty of poor stewardship with their resources and have gotten in over their heads. While they may need help, it would be a matter of judgment as to whether the church has such an obligation. Many might want to help in an emergency situation without making a long-

> For even when we were with you, we **commanded** you this: If anyone **will not work**, neither shall he **eat**.
>
> - 2 Thessalonians 3:10

term commitment. Such people might need some counseling about their finances so as to avoid future problems.

But, there are many circumstances which are totally out of someone's control, like major illnesses, tornadoes, a car accident, or a bad economy where jobs cannot be found. What is to be done then?

The Bible outlines a three step process to deal with such situations. The family has the first line of obligation, then individual Christians, and then, in the case of needy Christians, the church.

The family

The primary responsibility of caring for people has been placed on the family. "But if anyone does not provide for his own, and especially for those of his household, he has denied the faith and is worse than an unbeliever" (1 Timothy 5:8). This verse clearly places the duty of caring for one's own family on the man of the house. And note that those duties extend beyond those living under his own roof. It refers to "those of his household" and implies therefore that other family members, not of his own household, must also be cared for.

> If any **believing** man or woman has **widows**, let them **relieve** them, and do not let the **church** be **burdened**, that it may **relieve** those who are **really** widows.
>
> - 1 Timothy 5:16

That was the important lesson that Paul was teaching in the first sixteen verses of 1 Timothy 5, that family must take care of their own. Only a special, select group of women (they had to meet certain qualifications, just like elders do) could be cared for by the church on a regular basis. He called them "really widows" or "widows indeed" (in the King James Version).

Earthly family had the first obligation to care for widows. "If any believing man or woman has widows, let them relieve them, and do not let the church be burdened, that it may relieve those who are really widows" (1 Timothy 5:16). But those who were totally alone (verse 5, the King James uses the word "desolate" to describe them) could be cared for by the church.

The first question that ought to be asked following any benevolent request is "What about your family? Have you talked with them? Will they help you?"

Individual Christians

After it has been determined that family cannot or will not help a need, then it becomes the duty of individual Christians to help. Such help would include Christians and non-Christians alike.

"Therefore, as we have opportunity, let us do good to all, especially to those who are of the household of faith" (Galatians 6:10).

"Pure and undefiled religion before God and the Father is this: to visit orphans and widows in their trouble, and to keep oneself unspotted from the world" (James 1:27).

"If a brother or sister is naked and destitute of daily food, and one of you says to them, 'Depart in peace, be warmed and filled,' but you do not give them the things which are needed for the body, what does it profit?" (James 2:15-16).

We must have a heart of compassion for the needy and those who do not will be rejected by Christ in the final judgment (see Matthew 25:31-46). There will be far more needs than anyone can personally meet. But, as in all areas of service to God, our responsibilities are limited by our opportunities and our ability.

The church

When family and individual Christians have done what they can, then the church has an obligation to help. But every example of this in the Bible mentions only helping needy Christians, not non-Christians. (This, of course, has been one of the major points of division in the church in its recent past.)

There are three methods of "church benevolence" mentioned in the New Testament.

...for I was **hungry** and you gave Me **food**; I was **thirsty** and you gave Me **drink**; I was a **stranger** and you **took** Me in...

- Matthew 25:35

For it pleased those from **Macedonia** and **Achaia** to make a certain **contribution** for the **poor** among the **saints** who are in **Jerusalem**.

- Romans 15:26

1. *A congregation may take care of its own members.*

   In the Bible, when members were in need, the other members helped them, as they had the ability to do so (Acts 2:44-47; Acts 4:32-37; Acts 6:1-4).

2. *Other churches may send to one church that is unable to take care of its own members.*

   There are two such examples in the Bible. The churches of Macedonia and Achaia sent relief to the poor saints in Jerusalem (Romans 15:25-26). The Jerusalem church also received a contribution from the churches of Galatia and Corinth (1 Corinthians 16:1-2; 2 Corinthians 8 and 9).

3. *One church may send to many churches, if those churches have saints who are in need.*

   The church in Antioch sent to the churches in Judea (Acts 11:27-30). The relief was not sent to Jerusalem as the sponsoring church for the whole arrangement, but to the elders of each church in Judea for distribution. (Some of the towns in Judea which probably had churches would include Jerusalem, Joppa, Lydda, Emmaus and Bethany. The churches [plural] in Judea are mentioned in 1 Thessalonians 2:14).

What about 2 Corinthians 9:13?

We need to take a special look at 2 Corinthians 9:13 in this context. It reads like this: "While, through the proof of this ministry, they glorify God for the obedience of your confession to the gospel of Christ, and for your liberal sharing with them and all men." Some believe that this verse refers to benevolent help from the church in Corinth to both saint and sinner.

There are two important questions that will help us to understand the meaning of this passage. Why was the money collected and how was the money used?

1. *Why was the money collected?*

   Every verse that deals with the collection of these funds specifies that *saints* (Christians) were those who would receive the help.

   "Now concerning the collection *for the saints*, as I have given orders to the churches of Galatia, so you must do also" (1 Corinthians 16:1).

   "But now I am going to Jerusalem to minister *to the saints*. For it pleased those from Macedonia and Achaia to make a certain contribution for *the poor among the saints* who are in Jerusalem" (Romans 15:25-26).

   As noted, this money (or goods or clothes or food or whatever) was collected for needy Christians. Did Paul represent it as that and then distribute it to anyone and everyone who asked? Did he collect the funds for one purpose and use them for another?

   That brings us to the next question.

2. *How was the money used?*

   Space will not permit a complete listing of chapters 8 and 9 of 2 Corinthians. The student is encouraged to read the entire text of these two chapters. Please note these selected verses.

   - 8:4: "imploring us with much urgency that we would receive the gift and the fellowship of the ministering to the saints"

   - 8:14: "but by an equality, that now at this time your abundance may supply their lack, that their abundance also may supply your lack— that there may be equality"

   - 9:1: "Now concerning the ministering to the saints, it is superfluous for me to write to you"

   - 9:12: "For the administration of this service not only supplies the needs of the saints, but also is abounding through many thanksgivings to God"

It was in this setting that Paul mentioned this sharing with them and with all. (Notice that the word "men" was added by the translators.) This obviously speaks of Christians in Jerusalem ("them") and Christians in need in other places ("all"). These other Christians probably were those in the region of Judea around Jerusalem.

Conclusion

We know of no one who believes that needy people do not deserve help. The Bible clearly teaches that they do and that faithful Christians will help them. But we must be careful to do God's work in God's way and make certain that we are fulfilling our duties both individually and collectively, according to God's divine pattern.

Questions

1. Who should not get any benevolent help (2 Thessalonians 3:10-12)?

    _____

    _____

2. How important is it to God that we take care of our own families?

    _____

    _____

3. Read the qualifications of "widows indeed" (1 Timothy 5:9-10). Are there any you would like to discuss in class? _____

    _____

    _____

4. What are some important lessons we can learn from Matthew 25:31-46?

    _____

    _____

    _____

5. How much responsibility does each individual Christian have in the area of benevolence? _____

    _____

    _____

6. Discuss one example of each type of benevolent situation:
    A congregation may take care of its own members _____

    _____

    Other churches may send to one church that is unable to take care of its members _____

    _____

    One church may send to several churches _____

    _____

7. Explain 2 Corinthians 8:1-5. _____

_____

_____

8. What does 2 Corinthians 8:9 teach us about caring for others? _____

_____

_____

9. Discuss 2 Corinthians 9:5-7 in this connection._____

_____

_____

10. Do you know of any other scriptures which would authorize the church
    (collectively) to provide benevolent care for non-Christians? _____

_____

Two Misunderstood Passages

There are several key passages that have figured prominently in the division between liberal and conservative (or institutional and non-institutional) churches. We have already discussed a few of those verses in some of our previous studies.

Acts 11:27-30 has been misapplied by institutional brethren, who have claimed that it is an example of the sponsoring church arrangement. We discussed that passage in Lesson 7.

2 Corinthians 9:13 has been a source of controversy as to whether it applies to benevolence for Christians only or for both Christians and non-Christians. Lesson 10 included a study of this important text.

Historically, there have been two more passages which have resulted in much disagreement, debate and division. They are Galatians 6:10 and James 1:27. This study will focus on those two verses.

The key to understanding these verses lies in remembering the difference between the church and the individual Christian, as we studied together in Lesson 4. It is a serious error to take a passage dealing with the obligations of an individual Christian and try to apply those duties to the church collectively. Both Galatians 6:10 and James 1:27 apply to the individual Christian, not the church.

> Therefore, as we have **opportunity**, let us do **good** to **all**, especially to those who are of the **household of faith**.
>
> - Galatians 6:10

Galatians 6:10

"Therefore, as we have opportunity, let us do good to all, especially to those who are of the household of faith."

PLURAL PRONOUNS

Some claim that, because the letter was written to the churches of Galatia and because the plural (we) is used, this must refer to church action. But such is not the case. Notice a couple of examples.

"Or do you not know that as many of us as were baptized into Christ Jesus were baptized into His death? Therefore we were buried with Him through baptism into death, that just as Christ was raised from the dead by the glory of the Father, even so we also should walk in newness of life" (Romans 6:3-4). Did you see that he used plural pronouns here (us, we)? But he was speaking of something that "we" did one person at a time, as individuals, when we were baptized into Christ. The plural pronoun indicates that more than one person did this; but it does not follow that this is "church" action.

> For **we** must **all** appear before the **judgment** seat of Christ, that **each one** may receive the things done in the **body**, according to what **he** has done, whether **good** or **bad**.
>
> - 2 Corinthians 5:10

"For we must all appear before the judgment seat of Christ, that each one may receive the things done in the body, according to what he has done, whether good or bad" (2 Corinthians 5:10). Paul begins here by saying that "we" (plural) must appear before Christ in judgment. Does that mean we will appear as "church" groups? Obviously not, for he continues on to refer to the individual nature of this judgment. But he began by using the plural, meaning that more than one person (all of us, in fact) will stand before the Lord, but we will appear one at a time, not as churches. The plural pronoun indicates that more than one person will do this, but it does not follow that this means it is "the church."

LOOKING AT THE CONTEXT

We must note the context of a verse to reach the correct interpretation of its meaning. And Galatians 6:10 is clearly talking about individual Christians.

Going back to verses 1-2, he has encouraged us as Christians (those who are spiritual) to attempt to restore an erring brother. We are to help bear one another's burdens.

In verses 3-5, he reminds us that we must personally examine ourselves and our relationship with God in order to determine if we are faithful or if we are deceiving ourselves. Each one (that's the individual) must examine his own work and his own relationship with the Lord. Each one (that's the individual) must bear his own load.

In verse 6, he deals with the duty of each one to support those who are teaching them the truth.

"Sometimes it is objected by those who want to apply the teaching of this passage to congregations rather than individuals that 'Let him that is taught communicate unto him that teacheth in all good things,' if individually applied would justify individual support for teachers. But this is no objection for the Bible certainly teaches that individuals as well as congregations did support teachers and preachers of the Gospel. When the above passage is applied to the church—the congregation—a collective body of Christians it is wrested from its context or setting and misapplied" (Roy Cogdill, *Walking by Faith*, page 67).

In verses 7-9, he is obviously dealing with our individual duty to God to overcome the lusts of the flesh and walk by the Spirit. And, he says that no one must ever give up on his walk with the Lord. Verse 7 emphasizes "whatever a man sows," not the church. Verse 8 speaks of "he who sows to the flesh" and "he who sows to the Spirit," not the church. Verse 9 teaches us (as individuals) not to grow weary in doing good and encourages us not to "lose heart." That clearly means that Christians, personally and individually, should never give up serving the Lord. It is not speaking of the church.

And then, in the conclusion of this section of the text, verse 10 tells us one of the obligations we have as Christians, to help those who are less fortunate than we are. The verse includes all people, but

> But let each **one** examine his own **work**, and then he will have **rejoicing** in himself **alone**, and not in **another**.
>
> - Galatians 6:4

Pure and undefiled religion before God and the Father is this: to visit **orphans** and **widows** in their trouble, and to keep **oneself unspotted** from the **world**.

- James 1:27

emphasizes our duties to each other as Christians. It is not talking about what we do collectively, but what we must do personally. Other verses tell us who the church is to help and under what circumstances. This verse does not deal with church action.

James 1:27

"Pure and undefiled religion before God and the Father is this: to visit orphans and widows in their trouble, and to keep oneself unspotted from the world."

Another verse that is often misapplied to the church is this passage from the book of James. Again, a careful study of the context of this verse shows that James is talking about our personal devotion to God.

Let's go all the way back to verse 12 to note the setting for verse 27.

In verse 12, James tells us that "the man" (not the church) who endures temptation and comes through it pure and holy will receive the crown of life which the Lord has promised to those Christians (not to the church) who love and faithfully serve Him.

Verses 13-15 speak of the process through which Christians are tempted by the devil. God does not tempt "anyone" (that's the individual, no reference to the church there). "Each one" (again, the individual) is guilty of sin when he gives in to "his own desires" (that's not the church, but what tempts each person personally).

Verse 16 tells us, as Christians, to not be deceived by worldliness and the temporary pleasures that sin offers.

Verse 18 reminds us that we (Christians individually, not the church collectively) are "a kind of firstfruits of His creatures."

In verses 19-20, James tells Christians to listen carefully and not to give in to anger or wrath which will not produce God's righteousness in our lives.

Verse 21 tells us to receive God's word into our lives and, at the same time, to put away filthiness and ungodliness. This, James says, will "save your souls." Are we saved as individuals or as churches?

Verse 22 instructs Christians to put the gospel into action in their daily lives. "Be doers of the word and not hearers only, deceiving yourselves."

Verses 23-24 says that "anyone" (individual) who hears but does not do is like "a man" (not like a church) observing his face in a mirror, but ignoring what he sees.

Verse 25 tells people to look into the Bible and do it. "This one" (individual) will be blessed in what "he" (that's not the church either) does.

In verse 26, he emphasizes the importance of watching what we say. A Christian who does not bridle his tongue (keep it under control) is deceiving himself about his relationship to God and his (this one's) religion is empty and vain. That is not talking about the church, but about the individual.

And so is verse 27. A Christian, in practicing "pure and undefiled religion" must help orphans and widows in their trouble and keep "himself" (KJV) unspotted from the ungodliness of the world.

Verse 26 tells us one way to practice vain religion. Verse 27 tells us how to practice acceptable religion before God.

An institutional preacher once asked me, "What kind of religion is the church supposed to practice—vain religion or pure and undefiled religion?" He went on to answer for me and tell me that the church should practice pure, undefiled religion and that verse 27 shows us how to do that. My response, if he had waited for my reply, would have been that this passage doesn't answer his question. It doesn't speak of anything the church is to practice, only the Christian. He was asking the wrong question based on this text.

The whole chapter is speaking of the individual and his/her relationship to God. If you read the entirety of James chapter one, you will not find the church mentioned even once.

Conclusion

Failure to distinguish properly between the personal obligations of an individual Christian and biblical authority for the church to act has resulted in many churches of Christ and all human denominations getting involved in many unauthorized activities. Churches are involved in numerous improper activities which simply have nothing to do with the work of Christ's church and do not please the Lord. The next study will deal with the social gospel emphasis that many churches have adopted.

Questions

1. Why is it important to distinguish between duties of the Christian and the work of the church? _____

    _____

    _____

2. True or false? Plural pronouns (like us and we) always mean the church. Explain your answer._____

    _____

    _____

3. Is the examination of Galatians 6:3-5 individual or collective? _____

    _____

    _____

4. Explain, in your own words, how Galatians 6:6 could apply to the individual Christian._____

    _____

    _____

5. Is the reward of Galatians 6:7-9 individual or collective? _____

    _____

    _____

6. Is the instruction of Galatians 6:10 individual or collective? Explain your answer._____

    _____

    _____

7. Is the warning in James 1:13-15 about temptation, individual or collective? Explain your answer._____

    _____

    _____

8. Do you think James 1:21-25 is speaking to the individual or to the church? What makes you think that?_____

    _____

    _____

9. Could James 1:26 be applied to the church collectively? Explain your answer._____

_____

_____

10. What would lead one to conclude that James 1:27 is a collective responsibility?_____

_____

_____

The Social Gospel

Does the Lord's church have any social agenda? Certainly, the early Christians spent a lot of time together (Acts 2:46; Romans 12:13; 1 Peter 4:9). But did the early church sponsor those social get-togethers or were they simply a function or an extension of the Christian's home life? Did Jesus die on the cross so His followers could play softball or soccer on a church league team? Did the Son of God leave heaven so women could get together and exercise in a church gymnasium? Is the purpose of Christianity to provide a good, hot meal for disciples on a regular basis?

> So continuing **daily** with **one accord** in the temple, and **breaking bread** from **house to house**, they ate their food with **gladness** and **simplicity** of **heart**.
>
> - Acts 2:46

The work of the church, again

It is vitally important that we remember what is and what is not the work of the local church. There are many activities that are not a part of God's plan for the work of a local church, that are commonly practiced by religious denominations and by some churches of Christ. Here are some examples.

DAY CARE CENTERS

Child care is to be provided by the home. It is not the job of the Lord's church to babysit people's children for them. Like the other things listed here that are common social functions of many religious groups, this activity is not wrong or sinful, in and of itself. But what Bible verse or biblical principle would teach us that this is something the church should do? The church is not a babysitting service.

SECULAR SCHOOLS

The work of the church is spiritual, not secular. Churches are schools in the sense that they provide learning for students. But the subject is the word of God, not reading, writing, arithmetic, science, history or literature. See Matthew 28:18-20; Ephesians 4:11-16; 1 Timothy 3:15.

FOOD AND FUN

"The increasing tendency to socialize church services and church work by having 'fellowship banquets,' a social hour with refreshments after the service for various groups, a church dining room, parlor or cafeteria to entertain visitors and accommodate social functions, serving refreshments between Bible classes and worship to attract greater attendance is purely sectarian and leads directly to what Paul condemned upon the part of the Corinthians" (Roy Cogdill, *Walking by Faith*, page 8).

In 1 Corinthians 11:17-34, Paul deals with the problem of the Corinthian church improperly observing the Lord's Supper. They had turned it into an ordinary meal and were not even waiting for each other to eat. He corrects their misunderstanding about the important nature of the Lord's Supper and tells them to observe it together, not independently. Then he tells them that, if they want to eat a regular meal, they should do that at home, in other words, not as an approved "church function." Verse 22 says, "Do you not have houses to eat and drink in?" Verse 34 adds, "But if anyone is hungry, let him eat at home." Eating a meal together "as a church" (verse 18) was prohibited.

Romans 14:17 tells us that "...the kingdom of God is not food and drink, but righteousness and peace and joy in the Holy Spirit." They had the wrong emphasis and were told to focus on the spiritual.

John 6:1-14 is sometimes used as "proof" that the church can serve food and then use that occasion to preach to people. It actually teaches the opposite of that and condemns those who come only for "the food which perishes" (verses 26-27).

BALL TEAMS/SPORTS EVENTS

"It is not the business or work of the church to provide and serve as guide in recreational activity.

> What! Do you not have **houses** to **eat** and **drink** in?
>
> - 1 Corinthians 11:22

Church basketball teams, church sponsored skating parties and swimming parties, facilities for ping-pong games and the like are a perversion of the energies and resources of the church. It isn't the business of the church to provide entertainment or recreation for either young or old" (Cogdill, ibid., page 8).

SOCIAL ACTIVITIES FOR YOUNG PEOPLE

A lot of people today "choose a church" based on how many social activities that group will provide for their young people. Once again, everyone needs to be reminded that the work of the church is spiritual and that it is the duty of parents to provide social interaction for their children, and that can include lots of social times spent together doing lots of fun things. But the work of the church is not to supply fun and games for young people.

ADVANCING POLITICAL CAUSES

"Political issues do not belong in the church. God ordained civil government to meet all such issues and resolve them and they should be left there. Romans 13:1-7; 1 Peter 2:13-17" (Cogdill, ibid., page 9).

The problem is that many denominational churches have gotten involved in numerous activities that have nothing to do with the New Testament pattern. But they are so common and widespread that society has just come to expect churches to offer these kinds of things. And some brethren, wanting to be "like the nations around them," have decided to imitate these popular activities, even without any biblical authority.

Does the Bible promote social change?

What the Bible teaches as the primary work of the church is the saving of souls (and the worship of God; please review Lesson 5). This is done through the preaching and teaching of the gospel of the crucified and resurrected Christ (1 Corinthians 15:1-3).

"For I am not ashamed of the gospel of Christ, for it is the power of God to salvation for everyone who

> Let every **soul** be **subject** to the **governing authorities**. For there is no authority except from **God**, and the authorities that exist are **appointed** by God.
>
> - Romans 13:1

believes, for the Jew first and also for the Greek" (Romans 1:16). Only if one has lost faith in the gospel to convert people to the Lord would he even consider changing the mission of the church to a social agenda.

Notice 1 Corinthians 6:9-11. "Do you not know that the unrighteous will not inherit the kingdom of God? Do not be deceived. Neither fornicators, nor idolaters, nor adulterers, nor homosexuals, nor sodomites, nor thieves, nor covetous, nor drunkards, nor revilers, nor extortioners will inherit the kingdom of God. And such were some of you. But you were washed, but you were sanctified, but you were justified in the name of the Lord Jesus and by the Spirit of our God."

When they were converted by the gospel, these previous sinners gave up their sinful practices. Fornicators and adulterers stopped their immorality. Idolaters quit worshiping false gods. Homosexuals and sodomites gave up their illicit relationships. Thieves quit stealing. The greedy changed their covetous hearts. Drunkards stopped drinking. Revilers and extortioners abandoned their wicked ways.

But it wasn't because the early church set up social organizations to provide counseling for the ungodly. Society, however, was improved by these sinners giving up their evil deeds. But it was because of the power of the gospel to change lives, not some social agenda.

"Whatever impact it *(the gospel, rh)* was to have in correcting social evils was to be accomplished as a by-product of this transforming of individuals" (Sewell Hall, "The Impact of the 'Social Gospel' on the Church," *Guardian of Truth* magazine, January 2, 1986).

There are numerous Bible subjects that have both a social and a moral application. Abortion, drinking, family life, pornography, sexual immorality, and many other topics must be preached on so that Christians can learn God's will on those moral issues. But, the church must be careful not to cross a line into taking social action, rather than emphasizing spiritual responsibility toward God.

A step in the direction of modernism

In the denominational world, many religious groups have completely abandoned any pretense that they still believe the gospel message of the Bible will convert people to Christ. They believe that they must offer social activities as a part of the work of the church in order to keep people coming (and, in many cases, they are probably right). This phenomenon is commonly called modernism.

"In the great universities of Germany, scientific objections to the basic doctrines of the Christian faith gained such credence in intellectual circles that theologians were forced to re-examine their traditional views.

The historic creeds, which rested their claims to authority on the Holy Scriptures, were scrapped or reinterpreted in terms of evolutionary naturalism or divine immanence. Abandoned to the new culture were the inspiration of the Scriptures, the unique deity of Christ, the miracles, the atonement for sin, the bodily resurrection, the individual resurrection of the saints, the second coming of Christ unto final judgment, heaven, hell, and every vestige of the supernatural elements of the Christian faith. The mind of man was made the court of final appeal" (James DeForest Murch, *Christians Only*, page 224, quoted in *Guardian of Truth* magazine, January 2, 1986, in the article by Sewell Hall referenced earlier).

While most churches of Christ have not gone as far into the social gospel and modernism as described in this quote, any social gospel approach is a step in the wrong direction.

Numbers are proof

There are those who would reason that such social activities are justified on the basis of drawing a crowd that can then be taught the gospel. And they would point to large denominational or institutional groups that employ such tactics as proof that this approach works. But numbers are never proof of faithfulness or acceptability to God. To the contrary, the Bible shows repeatedly that the majority is often wrong (see Lesson 2 on how to determine if something pleases God).

It can be a very worldly viewpoint to simply want the church to grow for the sake of numbers and prestige. Our perspective must be that every number represents a soul won for God and not simply a chance to have a "bigger church."

The use of the church building

The only authority for even owning a church building in the first place is to provide a place to do what the Lord says a church should do. Hebrews 10:25 teaches that the church is to assemble together for worship and a place is authorized in that command.

...not **forsaking** the **assembling** of ourselves **together**, as is the manner of some, but **exhorting one another**, and so much the more as you see the **Day** approaching.

- Hebrews 10:25

One institutional church of Christ, in an article detailing the many social uses of their building, said, "Church buildings exist as tools for people to use in the pursuit of a better life. They are not monuments or objects of veneration. They are not sacred places subject to defilement by activities which may not have a hymn or prayer associated with them." They went on to list such weekly activities as Co-Dependency Survivors, Room in the Inn *(I don't even know what that is, rh)*, Ladies Exercise Group, Alcoholics Anonymous, Alanon, Divorce Recovery Group, Children's Tutoring, Adult Education, Nashville Christian Singles, and Narcotics Anonymous. Which Bible verses would you turn to in order to show Bible authority for these socially oriented group activities to be provided by the Lord's church?

First of all, the church building, paid for with the Lord's money, is to be used to accomplish His will. If these activities are scriptural, where does the Bible say so?

Secondly, the issue is not, and never has been, whether a church building is sacred and will be defiled by such. The only question really is, does God want His church to be involved in these things? The only way we could know that He does is if He has told us so (1 Corinthians 2:9-13). And, clearly, He has not.

Thirdly, church buildings are not tools to help people live a better life. They are tools to be used to help people in pursuit of eternal life with God in heaven. That's really what the church is all about.

The whole man

The argument is often made that the church has a duty to minister to "the whole man," and that this responsibility would include his social needs as well as his spiritual needs. That sounds good, but where does the Bible teach that? The church has a duty to worship God and to save souls. If there is an obligation to the whole man, where has God revealed that to us? That may seem like a pragmatic approach to church growth today, but our duty is to find God's will and do that—nothing more and nothing less.

Conclusion

"The real problems of the world are spiritual. The local church is God's organization for dealing with such problems and the gospel of Christ is the means He has given us with which to confront them. Ten thousand other organizations are addressing the social problems of our day, using every conceivable resource. It is urgent that we not allow ourselves to be distracted from our unique mission nor disillusioned with God's unique method" (Hall, ibid.).

Questions

1. What does the term "social gospel" mean to you?_____
    _____
    _____

2. Show with a few scriptures why you think the social gospel approach is right or wrong. _____
    _____
    _____

3. Discuss Romans 14:17 in connection with this study. _____
    _____
    _____

4. John 6:1-14 is sometimes quoted as proof that we can feed a group of people in order to have the chance to preach to them. Do you think this passage proves that? Why or why not? _____
    _____
    _____

5. Are we engaging in a social gospel approach when we preach about subjects like pornography, abortion, alcohol, etc.? Explain your answer.
    _____
    _____
    _____

6. What do you think of this statement? "Whatever impact it (the gospel) was to have in correcting social evils was to be accomplished as a by-product of this transforming of individuals."_____
    _____
    _____
    _____

7. List some of the primary tenets of Christianity abandoned by modernism (from the quote by Murch). _____
    _____
    _____
    _____

8. What is the relationship between a social gospel approach and an inappropriate emphasis on "numbers?" _____

    _____

    _____

    _____

9. Do you believe this statement? "Church buildings exist as tools for people to use in the pursuit of a better life. They are not monuments or objects of veneration. They are not sacred places subject to defilement by activities which may not have a hymn or prayer associated with them." Explain your answer. _____

    _____

    _____

    _____

10. A phrase often used in defense of social activities as a work of the church is that the church must minister to "the whole man." Do you agree or disagree and why? _____

    _____

    _____

    _____